T0149378

PHILOSOPHY WITH CHICKENS AND DUCKS

Scott Portsche

authorHOUSE®

AuthorHouse™
1663 Liberty Drive
Bloomington, IN 47403
www.authorhouse.com
Phone: 1 (800) 839-8640

Published by AuthorHouse 06/28/2019

ISBN: 978-1-5462-6882-6 (sc)
ISBN: 978-1-5462-6881-9 (e)

Library of Congress Control Number: 2019908756

Print information available on the last page.

This book is printed on acid-free paper.

I would like to dedicate my book to my mother, father, and brother.

THE TRUTH

Alone I sit in the darkness.
Below me the Earth, above me the Heavens.
Others have come before me with the same questions.
I do not sit on a pedestal, I am a mortal.
Serene silence envelopes me.
This is the calm before the storm.
Suddenly the air is filled with energy.
A fog dawns upon me.
Sparks of fire light up the aether as murky clouds roll in.
I am not alone.
The wind slowly whispers away.
There is silence once more.
Brilliant flashes shine understanding upon my eyes.
There is something ahead of me.
A figure clouded in the fog?
An unrelenting light?
The cryptic sound of words?
It yearns to be discovered.
I rise to my feet,
"I do not fear you."
I reach out,
"Why do you hide from me?"
My knees buckle as I fight forward.
"I will discover the truth."
I am so close, yet I am so far.

YOUR STORY

In a world that can be so beautiful yet so cruel,

You have created a story,

Made up of the best and worst of times,

Made up of family and their love,

Made up of accomplishments and journeys,

Made up of new beginnings and humble endings.

But what about the chances you missed,

The grudges you created,

The failures that have occurred,

The pains you have endured,

The difficulties you have experienced.

How will you remember your story that time has created and must end?

Will it be happily ever after,

Or a great disaster?

LIFE

This concept has bewildered humanity for ages.

What is the point of life?

When you give this idea great thought,

You are left with no answer.

Every time you wake up in the morning, there is no reason you do.

Simply put,

You begin your daily routine,

And continue your life among your other fellow worldly creations.

But what about the non-worldly realm that encompasses religion?

This idea of a final destination, home to perfection, gives man a point in life.

Skeptics may doubt the credibility of religion,

Yet religion has spread throughout man's world like a raging wildfire.

It gives humans a purpose and belonging in a mysterious universe.

Where our existence is not needed,

Yet it occurs,

And most importantly,

Provides us with a purpose that inspires us to wake up in the morning,

As life without a purpose isn't life at all.

REMEMBER

Stanley and Randy.

Who are they you may ask?

They are men forgotten in time.

They too once walked this earth.

They too once had families.

They too once read the words of authors.

But they are now forgotten souls among a galaxy of stars.

Some stars shine brighter than others while the forgotten hide in the shadows.

We as a people focus on the bright, but what about the dim?

Don't they hold as much significance as anybody?

For we are all stars that want to be,

Known,

Loved,

Remembered.

DEATH

Death contains more than just fear.
It is the answer to pain.
It is the answer to suffering.
It is the antonym of life.
It is unavoidable.
And yet, death is clouded with fear.

Many people do not want to live forever,
But what is the forbidden fruit that leads to this statement?
Death is a state of peace.
There is nothing to fear once death has occurred.

FORGOTTEN

A blacksmith pounds away at the glowing iron,

Raging with the light of a star,

Few have the skills and brawn to mold metal,

The heat gradually dies down,

Taking with it the intensity of the white flare,

The blacksmith grows old,

His work becomes brittle,

Both decay to dust,

Forgotten for eternity,

No remembrance to their name,

Who were they?

Nobody knows, yet they certainly existed,

What is the feeling of being forgotten?

ALONE

Such loneliness,
To feel this agony,
The soul simply disappears within your body,
The emptiness is profound,
It is a darkness within the mind.

Oh my God, my God,
I speak your name not in vain but rather despair,
What is this torture,
Sometimes I feel you leave me alone,
In this strange existence,
Are you there,
Yes you must be.

I dream of the future,
It fills me with joy and fortitude,
Suddenly it hits me,
Dreams are dreams and not reality,
Many have dreamed,
They now lay in the soil,
It's just a dream,
Reality is disappointing,
Certainly I cannot be alone in this realization.

CHANGE

As I lay motionless,
Unable to sleep,
My mind begins to wander.
I reminisce to a time not so long ago,
When I wondered what I would become when I reached the age
I am now.
By doing so my fears begin to unmask their forgotten faces.
The fears of my life changing for better or for worse.
These faces make me realize how quickly I have aged.
They make me realize the time that has passed me by.
Soon I will no longer live as a child,
In innocence and happiness.
Nevertheless,
Though I am proud of what I have become,
I am afraid of the change.
My life,
My world,
My family,
Will eventually all change.

BEING ALIVE

Humans are lucky to be alive,
Not in the traditional sense of survival,
Rather in the unique consciousness we possess,
Not a single animal embodies this idea of free will,
They are merely there,
They lack the spark;
With the wisdom and knowledge we possess,
We are unlike the feeble fauna that roam the Earth,
We are something more divine,
The masters of our domain;
Our awareness is unanimously a privilege,
To have this free will,
To recognize the abilities of our senses,
It makes us feel alive among the heathen creatures,
The savages that kill without consideration;
Pity the many innocents that will never get to experience this
privilege,
Carnage, destitution, negligence, ravage our world,
So precious is this life,
Yet we are utterly oblivious to its true value,
All because of free will.

WHAT IS THE PRESENT

The present is a deceiving concept.

Are you in the present even though everything you just read is in the past?

It is as if there are only the past and the future, but for a mere second, the present.

The present is not even within a mere second for within that second there is the past.

So what is the present, and is there a present at all?

There must be since you are currently reading this.

But what if the present is a combination of the future and the past?

What if the present is actually a moment from the future occurring and becoming the past.

Does that then mean there is no reality?

THE ETERNAL CHAIN OF POWER

The mighty shall fall,

So that the humble may rise,

Yet they too shall crumble,

As they are faced with almighty power and deceptive greed.

Soon a new successor will claim all of their glory,

And this cycle will repeat throughout eternity.

WEALTH

Every day a person dies,
From war, famine, and disease.
One day a famous person died,
And everybody lost their mind.

What kind of world do we live in,
Where we pity for those who have prospered,
And forget those who have suffered.

THE FOG OF WAR

On the thought of war,
Many jump straight to the soldiers on the frontlines,
Seeking to ensure the safety of their families back in their homeland,
Pioneering death upon the enemy,
As well as the government officials making the final decisions,
Demanding an enormous burden on their pawns,
For something they believe is justified with blood and violence,
Yet the people that are most affected are the citizens caught in the midst of all the chaos.
They lack the capability to fight back;
Their destinies are in the hands of pitiless brutes fighting a presumed demon on the other side of the bullet.

Far away,
Parents and friends remain,
And continue to persevere through their murky lives,
While their loved ones bleed out on foreign soil,
Their lives feel insignificant and wasted.

Loss is rampant in war.
Companionships and brotherhoods are shattered in the blink of an eye;
The voices of loved ones once in conversation fade away into the eerie abyss of the unknown.
A fog lingers over the towns, houses, fields.
Life will never be the same.

TIME FLIES

What makes time go by so fast when time is truly quite slow?

Is it the repetition or the joy,

Or the lack of self-awareness as the minutes tick by?

For example,

When an event will take place within a year,

Time tricks you into believing that it will take forever.

However,

You soon realize that the days, months, and that year have suddenly disappeared,

And all of the events you went through have become faint memories.

But is it an accomplishment to have made it,

Or rather a depressing realization of the quick duration of one's life?

GROWTH

Look at all I have lost as I have grown older,
Yet look at all I have gained.
With age, you become wiser and stronger,
Yet the people who taught you these lessons soon pass away.
And you are left behind.
Thus you must follow in their footsteps,
For it is your turn to raise the next generation.

NOSTALGIA

It's that time of year,
A cold chill brings warmth to my heart,
The static of my clothing flows electricity through me,
Classic tunes breathe joy into existence,
A familiar hot chocolate scent lingers in the air,
Faces shine genuine happiness,
Christmas only comes one time each year,
It's over as fast as it started...

The sun beats down upon ecstatic children,
People wander aimlessly, seemingly lost in surprise,
Slowly everybody disappears,
They leave behind a hum from a once lively building,
Another year in the books,
All that remains are the memories from the yearbook,
Where did the time go...

I am awakened in a foreign land,
The floor creaks beneath my feet,
It has aged well,
The sun beams a gentle light around the neighborhood,
The occasional car glides by relatively quietly,
Soon there are other relatives amidst me,
Grandma and Grandpa,
Father and Mother,
Greetings and conversation commence,
It is quite unlike anything else,
Time has taken it away from me...

Nostalgia does bring tears to my eyes.

CYCLE OF LIFE

Even in our mediocre lives,
We do not want anything to change.
When an everyday routine is altered,
We either openly accept it,
Or are disgruntled over its annoyance.
How can people find such beauty and security in their daily
cycles,
For those cycles will eventually change.
Nevertheless,
We must always enjoy our moments of achievement,
Our humble moments with family and friends,
Because they won't last forever,
But their memories will persist without end.

KNOWLEDGE

The story of Adam and Eve portrays the power of knowledge.
Before the forbidden fruit,
They lived in bliss serenity.
After the forbidden fruit,
They bore the weight of knowledge.
In the same way,
Powerful entities can create an illusion of freedom,
That prevents people from obtaining the truth of their subsistence.
Hiding knowledge from the citizens creates a stable society,
Similar to how our world is today.
Nobody will ever know the whole truth about our world.
In this way,
Knowledge is the forbidden fruit that gods try to hide from us.
Simply put,
Knowledge is power.

LEADERSHIP

A good leader can move a rock,
A great leader can move a mountain.

A good leader can unite the like-minded,
A great leader can unite the like-minded with the opposition.

A good leader can revolutionize an individual,
A great leader can revolutionize a nation.

A good leader can list the problems,
A great leader can solve the problems.

Do not be fooled by good leaders,
Be inspired by great leaders.

MAN

Modern society has created an interesting paradox,
Where we as humans do not constantly fear for our lives.
We do not understand how easy our lives are when compared
to that of animals.
Animals constantly watch out for predators.
A robin will raise its head in alarm to assure itself it is safe.
A rabbit will stop to listen astutely for predators.
Yet a human will continue on its way fearing nothing in its path,
For we have conquered nature.

THE LAST ONE

There were millions,
Then there were two,
And then there was one.

The silence seems louder than it ever was before,
The wind whistles more often now,
Waves crash against the shore.

Alone a hut stands among the foothills,
The tombstone not far away,
You are the last one,
There were millions before.

It is quiet; there is peace,
Yet there is unrest and discord,
Alone in a world with purpose no more.

The sun sets and the moon rises,
As it should,
Yet it feels like it should not,
Does time forget what it has taken away from me.

There is loneliness and remorse,
Just you and a horse,
In a land that has no end,
There is no other to befriend.

It is gone,

The past is far away,

The next day will come no matter what you say,

There is nothing you can change,

You are the last,

And you will soon fade away.

HUMAN NATURE OR NURTURE

Is a human natural,
Or is a human nurtured;
Give a human a lot of food,
They will grow burly and satisfied.
Give a human little food,
They will grow lean and ferocious;
Feral humans are incapable of reacclimating to society,
Language is taught rather than spontaneously obtained;
Take the DNA from a regular human being,
Raise a clone of it in a threatening environment,
The clone will become skittish and suspicious of all of their senses;
Put another clone in a peaceful environment,
The opposite will occur,
This human will become inviting and careless to danger,
They are both the same human,
Yet the similarities cease once one looks beyond appearance;
Which one of them is the real human?
Can these clones be defined as human?
Does personality stem from the environment or is it borne to one's self?
Is a human natural,
Or is a human nurtured?

UNDERSTANDING

In our lives,

We make assumptions that are based on limited knowledge.

The truth of the matter is,

You can't be cold if you've never been warm,

You can't be sad if you've never been happy,

You can't be right if you've never been wrong.

In this way, there is a system of checks and balances,

Where one must know the polar opposites of an idea,

Before they can reach a conclusion,

And judge a situation.

THE NOBODIES

You stand alone in the darkness,
Yet you have no fear,
While others ridicule you upon their pedestals,
You simply disappear.

Their egos blind them with a sense of security,
They feel that they truly have power.

They have none,
They are so easily manipulated by the nobodies,
History is written by the victors,
These victors are the nobodies,
If you do not know who they are then they have succeeded,
They alter the fate of the world behind the face of a leader.

There is no need for an eloquent voice,
A handsome face,
A magnificent stature.

All you need is a goal and an initiative,
And a way with words,
Then nothing will stand in your way as you blend in among the
pecking order.

Play along with the bliss and ignorant,
Those that think they are the lions,
Wait for them to stumble,
Infect them with your virus.

They will slowly deteriorate,
Your bidding will be done,
And once they have finally succumb to their disease,
You will have disappeared upon the breeze.

WHO ARE YOU

It is night.
I walk up to my window to peer into the darkness.
A figure grows larger and more clear as I approach.
It's me.
But who am I?
There is nothing really special about me.
I'm just like everybody else.
I'll most likely be a regular guy.
I used to dream as a child that I would be something else.
Of course, every other kid probably had those dreams too.
But when you get older,
Everything becomes more clear,
And you realize who you really are.

It is not the ending you want to believe,
But it is the ending that endures the trials of time.

PERFECTION

Does everybody truly think differently?

Politics is divided yet mankind is generally headed in one direction.

There is talk of equality, freedom, and unification.

Will government evolve to suit these needs?

Is there a form of government better than democracy waiting to be unveiled?

A great persuader can gather a large following.

All of these disciples generally think and believe the same fundamental thoughts.

We like to believe that each and every one of us is truly unique,

But what if we are all working towards one unified conclusion?

Some people miss a step here and there,

But overall society is progressing towards that one singular destination?

Philosophy, science, and the accessibility of literature are bridging the gaps.

All humans are learning the same fundamental ideas.

So where does it all end?

When will mankind reach the peak,

The limit of possibilities.

When will we reach perfection?

A LIFETIME

Look back,
One week ago.
How did you change?
You probably made a decision you'll end up regretting.
Look back,
One year ago.
How did you change?
You probably changed your view on a subject and became more mature.
Look back,
On a lifetime.
How did you change?
You grew over time into the person you would eventually become.
Time flew by.
Children were born and elders passed away.
You witnessed triumph and sorrow.
And in the end,
You endured the trials of life.

So looking back,
I hope you made the most of it.
Never forget to reminisce on your memories.
They provide lessons for guidance and allow you to remember the times of,
Love,
Joy,
And peace.

CONCLUSION

I am not all-knowing,

I do not think I have figured out life,

I am only human like the many that have come before asking the same questions,

Where am I in trying to understand?

I think there is a balance,

All around us, there is a balance,

Predator and prey,

Winter and summer,

Night and day,

Good and evil,

Life cannot function without this balance,

Humans cannot function without this balance,

We cannot constantly succeed or we would never feel accomplishment,

Our failures create desires, and fulfilling these desires completes one's self.

It appears in our world full of mystery there is no purpose,

Of course, there is religion but what of the man who lacks faith,

What keeps him on his steady course through life?

One might even ask why he is still alive?

Obviously, death is not desirable for anybody due to its uncertainty,

The poor are still here even in their current meager conditions,

Most continue to strive for something greater in this limited life,

Furthermore,

People say they live for their families, their future, their money,

Yet I do not believe anybody wakes up in the morning automatically thinking of those.

Instead,

We are so used to waking up and doing our daily routines that living is just normal.

Everybody lives in the present,

We forget that we are aging,

We forget that nothing lasts forever,

We do not realize how quickly the world is changing around us,

It is only until it is too late when we realize that five years have gone by,

Those five years are gone,

I have thought as a child what it would be like growing up,

Unlike many, I actually feared it,

Soon I would no longer be in the company of my brother and parents,

I would be alone for a while,

Maybe start a family,

And watch as my children experienced what I had during my childhood,

I would eventually grow old,

And no longer have the same ability to move and think,

But worst of all,

If I made it this far,

I would have to die,

At that age, you may think death is desirable,

But as aforementioned,

Nobody truly wants to endure it,

If I lived as I do now,

This thought of death would only happen every so often,

Otherwise, I would live in the present,

Worrying about what was currently affecting me,

But one night,

Lurking in my midsts,

Death would take me,

I would be gone,

People would not care,

Society would keep moving on without me,

How would my death truly alter their lifestyle?

You see,

Everybody lives in their own universe through their own eyes,

What affects them matters to them,

If something does not affect their everyday lifestyle,

Then it does not cross their thoughts,

Wars in far away countries do not affect your everyday farmer,

They may eventually,

Through the loss of a relative,

Or the increase in demand for their crop,

Otherwise, it won't matter to them.

Yet, at the center of all this talk is the everyday human,

With our divine knowledge and strength to conquer the unknown,

We create the lives we live,

The world would not be here without us,

How could there be a world without us?

The word exist was created by humans,

Thus the idea of existence was created by humans,

Without it, there would be no existence,

Our godly ability of consciousness gives everything around us existence.

We also have emotions,

Emotions give us that purpose to live for our families,

Even if we sometimes forget the true worth of our families by living in the present,

Likewise,

If a family member were to die,

We would care,

After all,

We knew them and the accompanying personality that made them human to us,

Once they are gone, life would certainly change,

We simply forget to recognize how brutally important they were until they leave us,
And realize we did not say our goodbyes.

I am not all-knowing,
I do not think I have figured out life,
I am only human like the many that have come before asking the same questions,
But this is what I know so far.

Printed in the United States
By Bookmasters